LOU-LOU

Poetry by Selima Hill

BOOKS

Saying Hello at the Station (Chatto & Windus, 1984)*
My Darling Camel (Chatto & Windus, 1988)*
The Accumulation of Small Acts of Kindness (Chatto & Windus, 1989)
A Little Book of Meat (Bloodaxe Books, 1993)
Trembling Hearts in the Bodies of Dogs: New & Selected Poems
    (Bloodaxe Books, 1994): includes work from titles asterisked above,
    the complete text of *The Accumulation of Small Acts of Kindness,*
    and a new collection, *Aeroplanes of the World*
Violet (Bloodaxe Books, 1997)
Bunny (Bloodaxe Books, 2001)
Portrait of My Lover as a Horse (Bloodaxe Books, 2002)
Lou-Lou (Bloodaxe Books, 2004)

CASSETTE

The Poetry Quartets: 2 (The British Council/Bloodaxe Books, 1998)
    [with Fleur Adcock, Carol Ann Duffy & U.A. Fanthorpe]

Selima Hill

Lou-Lou

BLOODAXE BOOKS

ISBN: 1 85224 671 5

First published 2004 by
Bloodaxe Books Ltd,
Highgreen,
Tarset,
Northumberland NE48 1RP.

www.bloodaxebooks.com
For further information about Bloodaxe titles
please visit our website or write to
the above address for a catalogue.

Bloodaxe Books Ltd acknowledges
the financial assistance of
Arts Council England, North East.

Cover printing by J. Thomson Colour Printers Ltd, Glasgow.

Printed in Great Britain by
Cromwell Press Ltd, Trowbridge, Wiltshire.

ACKNOWLEDGEMENTS

I would like to thank Andy Brown, Steve Cook, Stevie Davies,
Vicki Mackenzie, Helen Taylor and everyone at the Royal
Literary Fund and the School of English at the University
of Exeter for their patience and support during my time
as Fellow there – who knows what work the Devil would
have had for me otherwise?

*These poems are dedicated
to the memory of the late J.S.
and her waist-long, coal-black hair.*

Ward 6

They didn't have to touch us but they did.
They didn't have to bring us here
and wash us
and sit beside our pillows till the cry
of *Wakey, wakey, wakey, Little Ones!* –
'Little Ones' being us, enormous
blood-stained women
grunting on tin beds.

Night-room
JUNE 3RD

They didn't have to bring us here
and blind us
and lay us down
and leave us here like lumps
to rock inside this veil of white dots
we can't remember
how to understand.

Night-room
JUNE 12TH

People don't have faces anymore
and nothing here makes sense except pain
and everybody's here because they know
the only way to go is straight ahead
with nothing but a blanket
and the hush
of orifices opening and closing.

Night-room
JUNE 25TH

Leaving the vast and shimmering world behind me,
I find myself alone inside my hair
where, during the course of a million years or more,
tiny men with pointed hair like pins
come gliding in
in bead-encrusted ball-gowns.

Night-room

Our beautiful hush
is blown apart
by Sister
whose rigid breasts,
so sumptuous,
and belligerent,
whose smell of wild cats
show no mercy;
whose knotted muscles
and unruly hips
have no respect
for our austere unhappiness;
Sister, who strikes fear into our hearts,
who'll stay beside us to the very end,
uninvited,
with her juicy lips.

Night-room
JUNE 28TH

Here she is again,
the tiny woman
who drags a little suitcase round my head
and never succeeds
in catching up with the man
who glides ahead
in a pair of gold-rimmed spectacles
refusing
to acknowledge her small tears.

Night-room
JUNE 29TH

Leaving the world of arms and legs behind me,
I rock inside the forest of my hair
that grows and grows
until it fills the room
and hides me in its hush like a sock.

Night-room
JUNE 30TH

I know they think I ought to want my mother
but all I really want are the plains
on which to gallop
on the grandest horse
far beyond the window where she's waving,
dressed in a tiny, tear-stained, sequinned cardigan
with lines on her forehead which mean I am breaking her heart.

Night-room
JULY 1ST

When Sister smiles
she makes us feel like chocolate
being licked and softened by a tongue
that spends its life seeking out sweet surfaces
with which to share
its love of licks and licking.

Night-room
JULY 2ND

We're here because we like to keep things simple.
We like to think of nothing but ourselves.
This place is here for us.
This place is ours.
The nurses are all ours.
The drugs are ours.
All we have to do is do nothing.
All we have to do is ache with joy.

Night-room
JULY 2ND

Sister re-arranges us like lilies
taken from dark homes
and carried here,
crushed and precious,
to be sanctified.

Night-room

Sweeter and more frightening
than the indolence
I used to take my clothes off and surrender to
our summer afternoons at the piggery
that shimmered in the heat
like a palace
that wanted me to know
it was preparing for me –
me,
its brutal and voluptuous queen
whose hooded court
withheld their secrets from her
a little while longer,
just a little,
and only distant squeaks in the heat
told her something somewhere was alive –
sweeter and more frightening is the indolence
that fills the sunless hospital like syrup,
an indolence disturbed from time to time
by the distant squeaks
of a patient before her doctor.

Night-room

JULY 4TH

We have long forgotten our houses and our homes,
our pretty clothes,
our little dogs on leads –
we're not that kind of woman anymore.
We spend our days doing this now.
We never stop.
We do it all the time.
We smell not of ourselves but of each other,
of rubber gloves and borrowed dressing-gowns,
of rubber doors
endlessly opening and closing
and offering up and taking away the instruments
that chart the brittle world
we're being groomed for.

Night-room

JULY 4TH

We refuse to think about anyone but ourselves
and what we want
and how to feel pain
and how to avoid being herded into the day-room
where somebody's playing *Whiter Shade of Pale*
over and over again as if to say
leave me alone
so we leave her alone in her corner,
pressed in tears against the Dansette.

Night-room

JULY 9TH

We take our time to answer her,
like aeroplanes
who don't know how to move
or where to go
or how to understand that all she longs for
is eyes that look her squarely in the eye.

Night-room
JULY 10TH

We hide in toilets
like large flightless birds
that Sister insists on driving into the day-room.

Night-room
JULY 11TH

She claps her hands like castanets imploring me,
beseeching me,
her *darling*,
to wake up.
Things become transparent.
Underfoot
transparent sand goes *darling darling darling.*

Night-room
JULY 12TH

We creep about the ward at night
with sleeping pills nestling
in the pockets of our dressing-gowns
like the motherless eggs
of a sort of mutated insect
that doesn't know or care about tomorrow.

Night-room
JULY 12TH

The fact is we are stubborn.
We admit that.
And Sister has to come on bended knee
and beg us to respond,
just a little.
Just for her.
She pouts her crimson lips
and stares into our faces like a helicopter.

Night-room
JULY 12TH

The tiny man
that slides across my brain
is leaning over slightly to one side
like someone who has somehow ruined something,
someone else's entire life, for example.

Night-room
JULY 12TH

We shuffle to the toilet with our toilet-bags,
we chew our hands,
we open up our veins,
but nothing will deflect her from her task
of driving us like froth into the dayroom
where easy chairs line up like solid rock.

Night-room

Her smell alone is like a terrible accident –
burning rubber,
burning hair,
white spirit,
and blankets piled high like big grey roses.
One little sniff and nothing else will do.
Everywhere she goes she is adored.
Everything she touches turns to gold.
My hair itself
she turns to solid gold.
And the sound of her shoes on the lino's like goats from
       the mountains
that climb on our laps and nibble our noses and hair.
We need her right up close so we can smell her.
Our rows of little nostrils are aching.

Night-room
JULY 14TH

No one is allowed to come near us
or ask us how we are
except Sister –
Sister with her stiffened ginger hair,
her skin-tight dress,
her eyes like flashing lights;
who knows without a doubt there burns inside us
a golden sea,
on which she sets forth.

Night-room
JULY 14TH

All we know is something dark is moving.
We lie in bed and let her swab our veins.
We lie in bed and let the starry night
with its glittering upside-down watch
keep watching over us.

Night-room

Only the grandest pilots of eternity
are good enough for us,
of darkest night.
Visitors who stand beside our lockers
fiddling with their handbags,
please –
just go.

Day-room

It's seven o'clock in the day-room, time for Sister
to rattle her nails like bunches of music-stands
and drive our troupes of *loved ones*
meekly home.

Night-room
JULY 17TH

Our hairy blankets
nuzzle us like goats
who think our breasts
would make a nice jam.

Night-room
JULY 20TH

She's come from the ends of the earth
to call us Sunshine –
or, *one*, to call us Sunshine and then, *two*,
to stay with us and be with us always.

Day-room
JULY 20TH

She likes to sit beside us in the day-room
designing the beautiful dresses with matching handbags
we're going to model
on the Big Day,
and offering cups of coffee
to those visitors
who are finding it almost impossible not to collapse.

Day-room
JULY 21ST

We sit in rows and grunt
like warm pigs
somebody's dressed in poodle- and peach-coloured slippers.

Night-room
JULY 21ST

My scream
expands
like ballrooms
into which
the duty-doctor tiptoes with his needle.

Night-room
JULY 21ST

Above my head
the fingers
like warm slugs
that trace the cabbage roses
of the eiderdown
are trying yet again to befriend me.

Night-room
JULY 21ST

In the bedrooms of the very sick
tranquillised and isolated brains
rise and fall
like plastic bags on water
that spend their time
adopting strange shapes.

Night-room

JULY 22ND

Remember we are graceless, vicious creatures,
terrified of even being looked at,
but even we,
because of her,
succumb.
Succumb to what?
I want to say *to love.*
All I want to talk about is *love.*
I want to say *I thought it was all over.*

Night-room

JULY 22ND

She fills the night with blood
like a mouth
filling up with blood
you can't swallow.

Night-room
JULY 23RD

My little bed
is like a private desert
where even the sand
is made of nothing but ears.

Night-room
JULY 23RD

The gold and silver days of being no one
are stripping us of bone
like soft fish.

Day-room
JULY 25TH

She's looking at my hair
as if to say
where do we begin
but I don't know.

Day-room
JULY 25TH

Our visitors go home
as soon as possible
but even there
they hear our low grunts.

In a Hedge

JULY 25TH

This hedge
is like a nice airy tent
where I can take my overdose
in peace,
hidden from the prying eyes of those
who've chosen not to kill themselves today;
who walk about the streets as if it's easy,
as if they were *born*
to wear big shoes and clothes.
Well, I prefer to sit it out down here,
letting ants play havoc with my hair –
what used to be my hair
before the nurses
turned it into a sort of perfumed hat.
They thought it would cheer me up but it hasn't.
It's like having something alive on top of my head...
in the dusk the tall bony trees
glare at me as if I should be going...

Corridor
JULY 26TH

The next thing I remember is the light,
and lying on a trolley like a horse,
and someone holding out a sherbet lemon,
and not being able to close my fingers round it.

Office
JULY 26TH

My distant feet
like someone else's cattle
seem to be content
not to move.

Office

JULY 26TH

All I do is stare
and say nothing
and think *I'm sorry*
and *I don't know*
and watch a patient from another ward
shuffle in and try and sell us lipstick.

Corridor

JULY 27TH

Nurses lead us
to and fro
like horses –
the most beautiful horses
Sister has every seen –
thoroughbreds,
with legs like icicles,
and veins
pink fingers
daily flick and tap.

Day-room
JULY 28TH

They come to bring us hope,
which we despise,
then Sister comes
and drives them out again,
and indolence returns
like shimmering mud.
No one moves.
We are no longer human.

Day-room
AUGUST 1ST

Our visitors look down at their toes
as if they are ashamed
of what they know:
that hopelessness takes care of everything,
easily,
even suffering.

Bathroom
AUGUST 2ND

It's nearly dawn,
and raining,
when she finds me
alone on the floor of the bathroom kneeling in water.

Night-room
AUGUST 3RD

She hurtles through the ward like a train
hurtling through a land of sacks and walls.

Night-room

I know we look like sacks
but we're not,
we suffer night and day –
because of her.
We slice our little violet-coloured wrists,
we spray the walls with blood –
because of her.
We long to hear her footsteps in the corridor,
to see again
her cheeks, her flaming hair,
to smell her sheathed and undulating body
whose rectitude
strikes fear into our hearts;
which disappears,
even as we smell it,
even as we stretch our arms towards it,
disappears,
without a word to anyone,
in order to pursue its secret destiny
far beyond this dark we grip like roots.
Her little dress is tight
like a spoon.
Underneath her dress she smells of onions
softening in butter over gas.

Night-room
AUGUST 6TH

Our blankets lie on top of us like sheep
too dim to know
how desperately we love them.

Day-room
AUGUST 10TH

Beyond the zoo-like sloth of the humiliated,
whose brains,
like roses,
are falling apart in our hair,
she offers us,
her loved ones,
without pity,
bonds we can't believe we are afraid of –
after all, we are afraid of nothing –
the hot and muscular bonds of a love
no other love or lover has prepared us for –
bonds or rays,
brutal like the sun.
She bursts onto the ward like the sun.
Everyday she is our only sunrise.
She squeezes smiles out of us like resin.

Day-room

She ventures forth across the rippling lino
like someone with the world's only map
might venture forth across an unknown sea,
bound for distant islands where her little ones
will dance about all day getting married.
But we prefer to dream about our deaths.
We dream about our deaths all the time.
We dream about the hand of the stranger
covering our face with a sheet.

Day-room

Her voice is like a clutch of wild parrots
screaming to the doctors
from her hair.
They rush upstairs
to touch it in her office –
the hair, the belt, the tights,
they touch it all.
As for us,
all we do is ache,
like lambs in yards who ache for warm ewes.

Night-room
AUGUST 12TH

Now I'm up
I go from bed to bed
stealing people's sweets
for the orderlies.

Office
AUGUST 14TH

It's all arranged.
I'm going off the ward,
now I'm *so much better*,
with a nurse.
Three of us are going down together,
taking money with us,
and a list.

In the Canteen

I think about it all the time now.
I think about the bridge above the river;
I think about the fish
and the boats
and music in the air
and captains dancing;
I think about exactly what it feels like
to feel so wet you feel too wet to breathe.

Corridor
AUGUST 14TH

The visitors avoid the numb arm
that swings against their woollen coats
like rubber
as Sister guides me
back towards the night-room
and lets me down
like freshly-slaughtered cattle
only she
is qualified to handle.

Side-room
AUGUST 15TH

She locks us in
like whippets made of glass
whose life depends on learning how to pine.
By 'us' I mean the patients in the side-rooms
abandoned to our various long nights.

Side-room
AUGUST 18TH

I'm on the floor
in someone else's dressing-gown
trying to go upstairs and tell the doctors
to interview the fish in charge of drowning.

Side-room

AUGUST 18TH

I'm lying on my bed among the living
like someone made of gold with human hair.
The visitors are scared of me.
They look
then turn around and hurry swiftly home,
leaving me alone with my breaths,
grey and soft,
like moles in a wood.

Side-room

AUGUST 18TH

She tucks us in our beds
like wild swans
who tried to fly indoors
and bruised themselves.

Side-room
AUGUST 19TH

She wraps us up
like victims of infanticide
then goes downstairs
to *throw away our clothes.*

Side-room
AUGUST 20TH

The doctor disappears
like a goods train
that travels through the night without stopping
or caring who is born or who dies.

O.T. Room
AUGUST 22ND

Are you feeling better? I don't know
Where do you come from, Poppet? I don't know.
Would you like a coffee? I don't know.
I don't know this is it.
This is kindness
leading me back to the lights of my long-lost home.

Side-room

AUGUST 30TH

We spend our days lying on our beds
drifting down what feel like brown rivers
that carry us away to lonely palaces
disintegrating into deafening seas.

Night-room

AUGUST 31ST

Look, she says,
aren't they beautiful?
and so we are –
although they disagree
as they draw the covers over the beautiful scars
of the beautiful necks they probably want to strangle.

Night-room
SEPTEMBER 2ND

We *will not have* stray people on our beds
asking how we are:
we are not better.
And nobody and nothing must distract us
from lying on our beds
like marsupials
refusing to acknowledge they've been born.

Bathroom

Our glorious Sister,
like a summer day,
who never sleeps,
whose eyes are wide and scary,
who helps herself to people's grapes and chocolates
as they stare at their bedside lockers
and fall apart,
who is dragging a sleepy patient across the bathroom
to force her to open her eyes and admire my hair –
how sweet she smells,
how like an elephant
nibbling muffins in the afternoon.

Day-room

We like the way her hair is stiff
like cacti.
We like the way she's ruthless and severe.
We like the way she likes us as we are
and not as people think we ought to be.
Visitors may wave.
We don't wave back.
We're far too busy sinking into a torpor
that allows neither eating nor sleeping,
far less waving.

Day-room
SEPTEMBER 3RD

How fat we are,
how abject,
like old frogs
squatting on the feet of their beloved.

Corridor
SEPTEMBER 4TH

She lets us be as ill as we want,
and when we start to panic
there she is,
ready to receive us,
like a runway
made of blood by God to serve the sky.

Night-room

On quiet nights
we can hear the blood
pounding through her veins like God Himself –
God,
Who we refuse to be alarmed by,
Who all we really want's to be alone with,
and whisper to,
and find out where He's going,
in such a hurry,
in such strange disguises;
Who climbs into our beds and embraces us,
Who has no name,
Whose ears are soft and numberless,
Who rubs against our cheeks like Palaminos;
by Whom we are convinced we are adored.

Patients' Kitchen
SEPTEMBER 4TH

The doctors tiptoe primly past like dolls
but, once inside her room,
we hear them laughing –
throwing themselves against her desk and laughing.
No, *bellowing*, I mean, like dazzled bulls.

Night-room
SEPTEMBER 4TH

She breathes against my cheek
like a spoon
spooning something warm
into my brain
while far away
the days go by like barges
that have no heart
with which to know joy.

Office
SEPTEMBER 5TH

The bristly pigs
I loved to stuff with sandwiches
would press against my thighs
like the doctor pressed against me now,
but less discreetly.

Office
SEPTEMBER 5TH

The way I never speak
is like a mountainside
on whose white slopes
everyone is falling.

Office
SEPTEMBER 5TH

Sister is the only one whose touch
my skin can bear to be the object of.

Day-room
SEPTEMBER 6TH

She comes and stands beside us with that look
that means she loves us and she won't let go;
that means she loves us
of her own free will;
that means she has known and loved us
all our lives,
and is only keeping our promise,
as we must do –
and then she is gone,
and the ward sinks back into silence,
the silence of hearts that know *they can do no wrong.*

Night-room
SEPTEMBER 6TH

She's weaving in and out between our beds
like a lurcher with wings
in a sky full of cloud-dwelling rabbits
that can't resist not staying inside their clouds.

Day-room
SEPTEMBER 7TH

With chunky hair like handfuls of chopped jungle,
including chopped bromeliads and parrots,
she treats us like her tribe of *superbabies*
it's no use being less than ruthless with.

Day-room
SEPTEMBER 7TH

They smile at us
like they'd smile at sheep
they can't believe aren't bred
to smile back.

Night-room
SEPTEMBER 7TH

She's waving to us
from a long way off
like something waving
from a still lake
as if to tell us
as we fall asleep
never to forget
how much she loves us.

Night-room
SEPTEMBER 7TH

We dream of being ash inside white boxes
carried into offices by strangers
who carry in their other hands
our necklaces in paper bags
because we have no necks.

Side-room
SEPTEMBER 7TH

In the side-rooms
patients
like old horses
hang their heavy chocolate-coloured heads,
unaware
of rumours going round
that *razor-blades are on the ward again.*

Corridor

Tiny married women
gripping handbags
are regularly led onto the ward
and offered bits of cake
like birds on leads.
They cry to go back home.
Well they can't.
They've got to learn to love it here,
like we do,
and think of it as their *new home.*

Day-room
SEPTEMBER 9TH

Welcome to the wonderland of dreams,
of evening meals in the afternoon,
of plenty of time for the tropical flowers to bloom
that bloom in the night in the heads of the tranquillised sick.

Day-room
SEPTEMBER 10TH

The woman sitting next to me is smiling.
Apparently she killed a baby once
but now she's as serene as a potato
who's never seen a baby;
only mud.

Day-room
SEPTEMBER 12TH

Whenever they see my visitor
touch my hand,
patients look away,
as if pained.

Night-room
SEPTEMBER 12TH

Because I've started feeling *so much better*
I tidy my bedside locker
with little scratching noises.

Side-room
SEPTEMBER 15TH

Dressed not in a nightdress
but a dress,
I've come to visit D. in the side-room.
Look at her!
She sparkles like red glass!
She wonders if I'm going *near an offie*.

Sister's Kitchen

SEPTEMBER 16TH

However much he sits in Sister's kitchen
and lets her dare him touch my puffed-up hand,
however much she makes me *look my prettiest*,
I want them both to know *I'm not moving*.

Toilet

SEPTEMBER 17TH

Someone new arrived in the night,
her sobbing like a beautiful wet dress
in whose blue skirts
she wanted to be rolled.
She's sobbing now.
She wants to go back home.
Her hair is like a curtain of sardines.

Day-room
SEPTEMBER 18TH

Happy days are days she'll start the day
designing the dresses she wants us all to be wearing –
though *how will she ever get married,*
she wants to know,
if we never stop keeping her rushing around like this?
We blink at her
like gravy boats
whose brains
can only process *sleepiness* and *heat.*

Patients' Kitchen
SEPTEMBER 19TH

Take her away!
Take her away please, nurse!
How dare she come here bleeding in my office!
She claps her hands,
and then we hear the sound
of high-heeled shoes coming staggering down to the day-room.

Side-room
SEPTEMBER 20TH

The very weak,
becalmed in their side-rooms,
look forward to those moments
when I treat them
to glimpses of the brightly-coloured pill collection
I spend my days amassing in a sock.

In the Lift
SEPTEMBER 21ST

The little sobbing creature known as Sunshine
is asking me to help her with her shoes
but loops of snot keep getting in the way
and anyway
she isn't wearing any.

In the Grounds
SEPTEMBER 23RD

We're being taken out for little walks
in order to persuade us
that it's possible
to go for little walks without despair.

Night-room
SEPTEMBER 24TH

Too proud to even deign to turn my head,
the nights she comes and stands above my bed
as if she's come from plateaux of the moon
to meet my eye and force me
to acknowledge her,
I nevertheless get tempted to peep.

Night-room
SEPTEMBER 24TH

How beautiful she is,
how like an eiderdown
whose satin roses
thrive on polished night
like spaniels
emerging from brown lakes
caked in mud
and spangled with bright fish.

Day-room
SEPTEMBER 25TH

The folds and swellings of her sun-tanned body
smell as if she's come direct from Heaven
to stand before me in her uniform
and tell the others
shuffling to the bathroom
to come and see how beautiful I am
sitting – no, *enthroned* – in the day-room
underneath my crown of hair-sprayed hair.

Corridor
SEPTEMBER 25TH

Hasty movement doesn't suit my hair
so walking to the room where they're waiting
is taking me much longer than they planned.

Stairwell
SEPTEMBER 26TH

The visitors are coming up the stairs
and walking back and forth
with little parcels
for those they have to smile at
and wave at
and hope and pray will one day be more normal.

Reception

To the vision with tangerine eyebrows and rock-hard thighs
who appeared on the ward one night
when we least expected it
and proceeded to sail away
like the queen of night
down the rivers
and past the dark plantations
and out on the shimmering lakes of our hearts' desires;
who looked us in the eye as if she knew us,
as if it was time to go,
and we must get ready,
but who first demanded *everything* –
to her
we give not a word of thanks,
not a single smile,
as they lead us away to be normal,
hair-dos swaying.